Being a Financially Confident Woman
Every Day of the Year
by
Mary Hunt

4362-98

© 1996 By Mary Hunt
All rights reserved
Illustrations by Joel Barbee

Published by Broadman & Holman Publishers, Nashville, Tennessee
Printed in the USA

Scripture quotations are from the Contemporary English Version,
© American Bible Society 1991, 1992, used by permission.

Special Offer From *CHEAPSKATE MONTHLY*

What is *Cheapskate Monthly*?

Cheapskate Monthly is a twelve-page newsletter published twelve times a year. It is dedicated to helping those who are struggling to live within their means find practical and realistic solutions to their financial problems. *Cheapskate Monthly* provides hope, encouragement, inspiration, and motivation to individuals who are committed to financially responsible and debt-free living and provides the highest quality information and resources possible in a format exclusive of paid advertising. You will find *Cheapskate Monthly* filled with tips, humor, and just plain great information to help you stretch your dollars.

Turn The Page For Ordering Information!

How To Subscribe To *CHEAPSKATE MONTHLY*

Send check or money order for $15.95 (Canada: US Money Order of $21.95) to: Cheapskate Monthly
PO Box 2135
Paramount, CA 90723
(310) 630-8845

SPECIAL OFFER

Enclose this original coupon with your check or money order and your one-year subscription to *Cheapskate Monthly* will be automatically extended for an additional three months. That's 15 months for the price of 12! Such a deal, considering $15.95 for 12 full issues is already CHEAP!!

CALENDAR

JANUARY

1

THE BEST TIME to start saving money: 20 years ago.
The second best time: today! Happy New Year!

A BRAND NEW YEAR, fresh and unspoiled. Will you continue on the path you've traveled this year, or start down a brand new course? Now's the time to make a traveling plan!

EVERY WOMAN REGARDLESS of her marital status, age, strengths or weaknesses needs to know how to manage money confidently and effectively.

GIVEN THEIR TRADITIONAL savings and investing patterns, women who are retiring in the next 20 years will have less than 1/3 of the income needed to retire comfortably. — Oppenheimer Management Corporation

WHEN MONEY TALKS it often merely says "Good-bye." – Poor Richard's Almanac (1906)

DECEMBER

29

FIND PEACE knowing your life is in God's hands and that his timing will be perfect for you!

JANUARY

4

WORSHIP IS THE adoration, homage or veneration given to a deity. It's that deep, reverent kind of love we are supposed to reserve for God. Changing the focus of our worship from God to money is a very foolish thing to consider. It's very easy to allow money to become a god.

DECEMBER

28

L ET GOD STRETCH your imagination! "[God's] power at work in us can do far more than we dare ask or imagine!" — Ephesians 3:20

MY CREDIT CARDS gave me permission to buy things I didn't need, with money I didn't have, to impress people who didn't care.

DECEMBER

27

KEEP A STACK of postcards next to the phone to remind yourself it's cheaper to write than to make a long distance call.

JANUARY

Having the desire to make significant changes in the way you handle money is the key to becoming financially responsible.

DECEMBER

26

I CAN'T PROMISE YOU that getting out of debt will be easy, but it will certainly simplify your life!

Get a leg up on runs. Try this: Wash new pantyhose and allow them to drip-dry. Mix two cups ordinary table salt with one gallon water and immerse pantyhose. Soak for three hours, rinse in cold water and drip-dry. The salt toughens the fibers so they are more resistant to snags and runs.

DECEMBER

25

"For many, Christmas is the best night and day of any in the year. When it is finally over there's a wonderful exhaustion, a kind of lovely letdown, softened by the knowledge that it will all come again next year."

— David E. Monn, author

How YOU DEAL with money (your money habits) is determined by what you think about money (your money beliefs). Your money behavior is an outward display of what you believe about money and its role in your life.

THINKING RIGHT THOUGHTS that lead to right action is what wisdom is all about. When we come to know the holy God who is the creator behind everything we see and touch then we begin thinking right thoughts. Right living will follow.

Financial bondage is the result of being preoccupied with money—either from a lack or from an abundance. "Lord, I'm not asking to win the lottery and I'm not seeking poverty either. Just give me enough so that I am not constantly worrying about finances, but not so much that I forget to always rely on you." Amen.

GIFTS FROM THE kitchen deserve special consideration because for almost everyone, food equals love and that of course is what Christmas is all about!

WHEN A FOOL goes shopping the storekeepers rejoice. – Yiddish Proverb

GIFT idea: Fill an old cookie jar (whimsical, beautiful, or simply functional) with your own home baked cookies. Write out the recipe on a card and attach it to the jar.

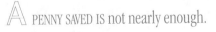

A PENNY SAVED IS not nearly enough.

TIRED OF THROWING out soggy, droopy celery? Cut off the bottom of the stalk and separate ribs. Fill a pan with cold water and stir in 3/4 cup sugar. Let celery soak for four or five hours. Drain well and refrigerate.

WE ARE WHAT we repeatedly do. Excellence then is not an act but a habit. – Aristotle

NOT FINISHED SHOPPING? Try to shop early in the morning when you are fresh, the sales people are less tired and stocks are less depleted, and don't forget your spending limits.

"A GOOD REPUTATION and respect are worth much more than silver and gold." Proverbs 22:1

DECEMBER

19

DEAR FATHER, All I have needed your hand has provided. Great is thy faithfulness!

JANUARY

14

Even when you fall flat on your face you've progressed by at least five feet! — Ron Jackson

SINGLE WOMEN SAVE only 1.5 percent of their annual income compared to 3.1 percent for single men.
— Oppenheimer Funds and A.D. Little/WEFA Survey, 1993

MONEY IS A tool that God gives to us—all of us, men and women alike—because He is the giver of skills and abilities.

THE EYE BECOMES magically selective during the Christmas season. Worn carpets recede, tired furniture appears warm and inviting and all that is festive and bright comes to the fore and homes are transformed. Enjoy the season!

JANUARY

16

Anyone who says money can't buy happiness has never bought new carpeting or a new car, or seen the look on a child's face on Christmas morning. The frustrating thing is that this kind of happiness is temporary. It quickly wears off.

DECEMBER

16

BEFORE YOU START your holiday shopping, set a definite spending limit which includes gifts, wrapping, mailing, and entertaining. Now discipline yourself to do whatever it takes to stay within that limit.

CONTENTMENT HAS A way of quieting insatiable desires. Contentment is the best antidote for an overly needy ego. Contentment comes when finally we fill that empty, hollow, longing in our souls with the only thing that fits perfectly: God whom we can know through his son, Jesus Christ.

Rules to Live By. Rule #1: Don't sweat the small stuff. Rule #2: It's all small stuff.

"YOU CREATED ME and put me together. Make me wise enough to learn what you have commanded."
Psalm 119:73

WHOEVER HAS A heart full of love always has something to give. Instead of a purchased gift this year, give your own custom coupon for something you do well such as running errands, baking a special dessert or a weekend of babysitting.

COFFEE MAKERS WITH built-in timers can be very expensive, so make your own for a fraction of the price: Purchase an automatic timer (normally used to turn lamps on and off automatically) at your home improvement center. Plug your coffee maker into the timer and for about $10 you'll have a coffee maker with a timer.

DECEMBER

13

IF YOUR GIFT list is getting too long, agree with friends and relatives to give gifts only to the children. You'll be amazed at how many others will feel relieved at this suggestion.

THERE ARE ONLY three ways to improve your financial situation: Earn more, spend less or sell assets to raise cash. Of the three, spending less is the least painful because you see instant results in after-tax dollars.

DECEMBER

12

G IVE YOURSELF the gift of a bill-free January! Shop with cash.

THE NEXT TIME you look in your closet and feel like throwing yourself a pity party, remember of all the things you wear your expression is the most important. If someone remembers your outfit and not your smile, you didn't smile enough.

WHATEVER IS USED to tie a gift should be saved and reused. Wherever possible, ribbon, cords, tags or cards should not be discarded. There are all kinds of ways to recycle them beautifully!

JANUARY

22

ALWAYS DO RIGHT. This will gratify some people and astonish the rest. – Mark Twain

CHRISTMAS LETS US see all over again how special people are.

A GREAT WAY TO start saving money: Stop spending coins. Even if the bill comes to $4.02, hand over $5 and rejoice because that means you have $.98 change to deposit into your change jar at the end of the day. Continue every day for about three weeks and you will have picked up a very valuable new habit.

Make some of your gifts this year. Fill small plastic bags with your homegrown dried herbs and tie with ribbon. Or put flower seeds from your garden in small, pretty envelopes. The ideas are unlimited.

"THE MAGIC OF compounding interest is truly the eighth wonder of the world!" – Albert Einstein

CHRISTMAS CUBES: To make festive ice cubes for cool drinks, fill ice cube trays halfway with water. Float a washed holly leaf or cranberry on top and freeze. Then fill trays to top and freeze again.

JANUARY

25

"EVERY WOMAN SHOULD have a purse of her own."
– Judith Briles

DECEMBER

7

I'T'S A WRAP! Use a roadmap to wrap up a gift for the traveler. Wrap a box in a piece of fabric or a pretty scarf. The Sunday comic section makes great gift wrapping for kids and teenagers.

How to Unshrink Wool. Mix a solution of one gallon lukewarm water and two tablespoons baby shampoo. Soak the garment for about ten minutes. Don't rinse! Simply blot out all of the excess water with a dry towel and very gently lay it flat on a fresh towel. Reshape slowly and carefully until it stretches back to its original size. Dry out of direct sunlight or heat.

THE BEST hot chocolate mix: In a large container mix together 1 8-quart box Carnation non-fat dry milk, 1 16-ounce box confectioners sugar, 1 28-ounce jar creamer non-dairy coffee creamer and 1 28-ounce can Hershey's Chocolate Milk Mix. To use place 1/2 cup mix in mug and fill with boiling water. Store in tightly sealed container.

WHEN IT COMES to those pre-approved credit card applications, remember what the big print giveth the small print taketh away.

INSTEAD OF PAYING $30 or more for a pizza stone, make your own for less than $2. Pick up one or two large unsealed terra-cotta tiles at your home improvement store. Place it/them on the lowest oven rack, heat oven to 475–500 degrees and place pizza directly on the stone. You'll be thrilled with the results.

FIRST YOU CHANGE your attitude, then you change
your life!

"You, Lord, are my shepherd, I will never be in need…I may walk though valleys as dark as death but I won't be afraid. You are with me and your shepherd's rod makes me feel safe." Psalm 23:1,4

WHEN OPENING A new container of milk, drop in a pinch of salt, replace the lid and give it a shake or two. This retards the growth of bacteria and greatly extends the milk's useful life.

"A PROBLEM WELL STATED is a problem half solved." — Charles F. Kettering

JANUARY

"KNOWLEDGE WITHOUT ACTION is like snow on a hot stove." – Ancient Proverb

I BELIEVE THAT WE should give away 10 percent, save 10 ten percent and create the best lifestyle possible on 80 percent of our income. "I know the best thing we can do is to always enjoy life, because God's gift to us is the happiness we get from our food and drink and from the work we do." Ecclesiastes 3:12–13

IF YOU DON'T change the direction you're going, you'll end up where you're headed.

DECEMBER

"LORD, I offer my life to you, everything I've been through–use it for your glory; Lord I offer my days to you lifting my praise to you, as a living sacrifice–Lord I offer you my life!" — Claire Cloninger

I'T'S THE LITTLE things that count and when ignored will sabotage your very best financial intentions. Keeping a daily record of where your money goes is the best way to keep your eye on all of those little things.

NOVEMBER

"WITH ALL MY HEART I praise the Lord, and with all that I am I praise his holy name!" Psalm 103:1

FEBRUARY

2

These days every woman needs to be a savvy spender, educated investor and successful saver because 85 of every 100 American women now age 32 will be on their own financially at some point in their lives: 6 will never marry, 33 will see their first marriages end in divorce and 46 will outlive their husbands.

NOVEMBER

29

OUR BUYING USUALLY reflects our value systems.

FEBRUARY

3

THE SECRET OF successful money management is not found in having more money but in wisely managing what you already have.

"CHARM CAN BE deceiving and beauty fades away,
but a woman who honors the Lord deserves to be praised."
Proverbs 31:30

IF FINANCIAL TRAUMA hits you month after month it's likely you are way out of balance. And more likely that you pay your bills first and if there's any money left over you save some and give some away. The way to get into financial balance is to follow these three simple rules: Pay God first, pay yourself second and pay others third.

DOES YOUR LIFE situation seem particularly hopeless today? Watch soap operas. By comparison your life will look like the proverbial bed of roses.

5

STOP! Don't throw out that ailing houseplant. Give it two tablespoons of Geritol twice a week for three months. New leaves should begin to grow within the first month.

NOVEMBER 26

THE WILL to persevere in the face of obstacles is often the difference between success and failure.

EVERY FAMILY NEEDS one good, all-purpose credit card in this day of high technology. It should have no annual fee and at least a 25-day grace period. If it is used during the month, pay the entire balance during the grace period so that you never incur an interest charge. A credit card should be a tool ... not a noose!

"IF YOU DON'T KNOW where you are going, every road will get you nowhere." — Henry Kissinger

"IF I CAN be content with little, then enough is the same as a feast." — Jamie Anne Warren, Cheapskate Monthly Reader

LIVING ABUNDANTLY doesn't mean acquiring everything we possibly can. For me abundant living has come as the result of finding my contentment in knowing that God loves me, finding money to be a non-issue so that I don't have to think about it much, and the personal freedom to need the things I want.

DON'T FIND ANY place in Scripture where women are relieved of the responsibility to be wise money managers. I don't know of a verse that says men are to handle the money. God requires all people, men and women alike, to be good stewards, to work hard, to make wise decisions, to give back to Him and to save for the future. Financial responsibility is for all of us.

"A TRIFLING DEBT MAKES a man your debtor; a large one makes him your enemy." — Seneca

"A TRULY GOOD WIFE is the most precious treasure a man can find! Her husband depends on her and she never lets him down." Proverbs 31: 10–11

WOMEN NOW MAKE up 51 percent of the U.S. work force and 38 percent of all shareholders.

A WOMAN WHO has never been exposed to the subject of money management is typically afraid of making financial decisions, doesn't feel capable and doesn't feel she can trust herself to make changes. She'd just as soon someone else make all of the financial decisions for her.

GLORIA, I'm not sure we can afford to save this kind of money.

FEBRUARY

11

FINANCIALLY CONFIDENT WOMEN regularly balance their checkbooks.

"INTEREST WORKS NIGHT and day, in fair weather and foul. It gnaws at a [wo]man's substance with invisible teeth." — Henry Ward Beecher

TYPICALLY, one of the two partners in a marriage is more naturally gifted with numbers. Terrific! Then that person should keep the records but not make all the decisions.

NOVEMBER

19

NEVER BORROW MONEY in anticipation of receiving a bonus, tax refund or raise.

NEVER CONSIDER YOURSELF a second-class citizen if you don't happen to earn a separate paycheck.

"DON'T JUST LET debt happen to you. Look at its true cost and at all the financial alternatives every time you borrow." — Andrew Feinberg, author

THE SCRIPTURES SAY, "Love the Lord your God with all your heart, soul, strength, and mind." They also say, "Love your neighbors as much as you love yourself." Luke 10:27

"It's WHAT YOU learn after you've learned it all that counts." — John Wooden

FEBRUARY

15

IT IS POSSIBLE to be responsible and fun-loving,
contemporary and spontaneous. Responsibility simply
means being accountable and that is a good thing.

NOVEMBER

16

"COURAGE IS GRACE under pressure."
— Ernest Hemingway

FEBRUARY

16

"BETTER A LITTLE caution than a great regret." –
Ancient proverb

THERE IS WISDOM in letting go of things that clutter and choke our lives. Junkees are the ones with a tendency to load up plates, places, vaults, homes, and conversation with more than is needed. The solution is simple: *De-junk your home, your car, your purse—your life!*

FEBRUARY

17

THE BELIEFS and therefore the attitudes you have
about money have a lot to do with why you always spend
more money than you have, why you don't believe you will
ever get ahead, why you feel so controlled by your finances,
why you can't get enough money or believe you don't
deserve much.

"IT'S NOT WHAT happens to you, it's what you do about it." — W. Mitchell

18

OLD PANTYHOSE make great substitutes for paint-brushes. Ball up the panty hose and use it like a sponge or secure it to a stick with several rubber bands.

TREAT YOUR COMMITMENT to giving and saving as you do your rent or mortgage payment. Make up payment coupons and addressed, stamped envelopes and place them in the front of your bills-to-be-paid drawer or folder.

ONCE YOU ACCEPT the fact that perhaps some of the things you believe about money might be defective or downright false you will be able to let go of old beliefs that keep you stuck in either hating or worshipping money.

12

IT IS MORE important for you to start to do the right thing than it is to wait until you think you can do it just right.

NEED RISES WITH income. What was out of the question when you made $25,000 becomes urgent at $40,000 and indispensable at $70,000.

— Jane Bryant Quinn

EXPERIENCE IS WHAT you get when you expected something else.

WHEN YOU START an investment program the jigsaw puzzle lies in dozens of pieces all mixed up. When you finish the picture will be clear and beautiful.

NOVEMBER

"THE SIGNIFICANT PROBLEMS we face cannot be solved at the same level of thinking we were at when we created them." — Albert Einstein

"THERE IS NO DIGNITY quite so impressive and no independence quite so important as living within your means." – Calvin Coolidge

CHOOSING TO PAY yourself before your creditors may be very difficult in the beginning. Paying yourself (even one dollar from your paycheck or household allowance taken off the top for you) cracks the door to a wonderful new habit.

A TAXPAYER IS SOMEONE who doesn't have to take a
civil service examination to work for the government.
— Stock Trader's Almanac

"THE FUTURE BELONGS to those who believe in the beauty of their dreams." — Eleanor Roosevelt

To REMOVE GREASE stains from linen, spray WD-40 directly on the stain, rub it in, let it soak for a few minutes then wash through a regular cycle.

A CHEAPSKATE GIVES GENEROUSLY, saves regularly and never spends more money than she has.

25

"I HAVE NO IDEA how much my interest rate is," says Suzanne Carver, a Chicago housewife as she paws through her purse to check her card. "It doesn't say on here. Well, as long as I can buy things with it, who cares?" – The Wall Street Journal, March 19, 1987.

ALL-PURPOSE HOUSEHOLD CLEANER: In a large container combine 1/2 cup white vinegar, 1 cup household ammonia, 1/4 cup baking soda and 1 gallon lukewarm water. Use in a spray bottle. No rinsing necessary.

It's DARING AND challenging to be young and poor, but never to be old and poor. Whatever resources of good health, character and fortitude you bring to retirement, remember also to bring money.

ELVIS NEVER TOOK a tax deduction for any of the millions he gave to charity. He felt it violated the spirit of giving.

BLAMING money, or the lack of it, for our problems and behaviors is no different than blaming others or God for our misery. We choose the role money plays in our lives and taking responsibility for that is the first step in making necessary changes.

As PART OF your program to get a head start on Christmas, make Mother Nature your partner. Preserve things from the garden or make your own infused oils and vinegars. Start now and you'll be ahead of the game.

Money can be as powerful a mood changer as the most potent tranquilizer — and as habit-forming.

Do you recall your thoughts of last December 23 or so? It was likely, "Next year I'm going to start sooner." Remember there's a tradeoff between time and money—the later it is the likelier you are to spend more. Today's a great day to get started.

FEBRUARY 29

GIVING IS AN EXPRESSION of my gratitude, a drain
for my greed, and the way I keep my life in balance.

2

TAKE GOOD CARE of what you have. Replacement can be costly.

MARCH

1

UNSECURED DEBT HAS a unique ability to destroy wealth, damage relationships, and dispel joy when it ceases being a tool and becomes a noose. "The poor are ruled by the rich and those who borrow are slaves of moneylenders." Proverbs 22:7

THE FINANCIALLY CONFIDENT woman's actions are based upon principles not feelings.

2

Enjoy what you have! "It's better to enjoy what we have than to always want something else, because that makes no more sense than chasing the wind." Ecclesiastes 6:9

"IF YOU GIVE to others, you will be given a full amount in return...the way you treat others is the way you will be treated." Luke 6:38

MARCH

THE FAILURE TO PLAN financially is one of the riskiest gambles a woman can take. "Without good advice everything goes wrong—it takes careful planning for things to go right." Proverbs 15:22

WHILE IT IS slowly closing, the wage gap still exists in this country. Women earn seventy-four cents for every dollar earned by men. That alone is a good argument for why women, above all, need to possess excellent financial planning and management skills.

"'TIS A GIFT to be simple, 'tis a gift to be free,
'Tis a gift to come down where we ought to be
And when we find ourselves in the place that's right
'Twill be in the valley of love and delight."
— Nineteenth Century Shaker Hymn

It's BETTER TO pay $300 for a suit you'll wear 200 times than $50 for a frock you'll wear once.

WHEN YOU NEED ADVICE, ask someone who's done it successfully.

28

THERE IS NO real excellence in all this world which can be separated from right living. — David Starr Jordan

⁶⁶**D**ON'T WORRY AND ask yourselves, 'Will we have anything to eat? Will we have anything to drink? Will we have any clothes to wear?' Only people who don't know God are always worrying about such things. Your Father in heaven knows that you need all of these .... Don't worry about tomorrow ...." Matthew 6: 31–34

SAVING MONEY IS the simple process of amassing money. Other than earning small amounts of interest, saving is an inactive process. Saving means never having to expose money to risk. Of course you don't expose it to reward, either.

Money management needs to become as important in your life as all the other skills you've learned. A financially confident woman is a woman who has the knowledge, ability, and desire to behave in a financially responsible manner. The designation is available to anyone.

WOMEN SAVE ONLY half of what men do on average.
— The Oppenheimer Management Report, 1992.

No SELLER HAS the right to my money without my full consent.

STOP RINSING AND prewashing your dishes and let your dishwasher do what it was made to do—rinse, scrub, clean, rinse again, sanitize and dry your dirty dishes. You'll be rewarded with a lower water bill.

"GOD IS GOOD. So I beg of you to offer your bodies to him as a living sacrifice, pure and pleasing. That's the most sensible way to serve God. Don't be like the people of this world, but let God change the way you think. Then you will know how to do everything that is good and pleasing to him." Romans 12:1–2

ABOUT 30 PERCENT of the energy spent in the typical home is used for water heating.

MARCH

10

Don't fool yourself into thinking challenges of a financial nature will never come upon you and your family.

SOLVENCY IS THAT confident feeling of being prepared for any circumstance, of living with joy and peace–of living with dignity and within your means at all times.

MARCH

11

DON'T LOOK UPON your credit limit as part of your income or an entitlement to have what you cannot afford with your regular income.

OCTOBER

22

"Do what the Lord wants and he will give you your heart's desire." Psalm 37:4

MARCH

12

"WHEN WE WERE CHILDREN we thought and reasoned as children do. But when we grew up, we quit our childish ways." I Corinthians 13:11

OCTOBER

21

THE GOOD NEWS is that no matter what level of debt you find yourself there is a way to successfully control, reverse and dig your way out once and for all.

"IT IS NEVER TOO LATE to be what you might have been." — George Elite

OCTOBER

20

No MATTER WHAT your present situation, there's always a way out.

MARCH

14

Have nothing in your home that you do not know
to be useful and believe to be beautiful.

OCTOBER

19

REMOVE STAINS FROM marble with a paste made of baking soda and white vinegar.

WHY IS IT that banks lend money only to those who have it?

AVOID OVERDUE FINES at the library. Most libraries will renew books over the phone.

"STYLE HAS NOTHING to do with money. Anybody can do it with money. The true art is to do it on a shoestring."
— Tom Hogan

"AFFLUENT FOLKS ARE those who earn money and manage to hang onto it by spending less than they make."
— Paul A. Merriman

"THERE NEVER HAS been a house so bad that it couldn't be made over into something worthwhile."
— Elsie de Wolff

FOR EVERY $1 you have you can only part with it once. You can spend it or you can save it.

Tin Lily

No matter how difficult your situation, get creative
and bloom where you're planted.

OCTOBER

15

SEPARATE YOUR NEEDS from your wants.

THERE ARE SOME THINGS you learn best in calm and some in storm.

THREE SIMPLE LIFE insurance rules:
1. It's not for you. It's for the people you will leave behind.
2. Keep it simple. Clean and easy policies are the surest.
3. Be a cheapskate. Buy the lowest-cost life insurance policy you can find.

WHEN IT COMES to spending money, for each "yes" there must be a "no."

WHEN YOUR LUCK is down and your world goes wrong,
When life's all uphill and the road is long—
Keep your spirits high for through thick and thin—
You must carry on if you are to win.
Never mind if things slow you down a bit;
You'll come out on top—but you mustn't quit
— Author Unknown

MARCH

21

DON'T WORRY—be happy! "Don't worry about anything but pray about everything." Philippians 4:6

OCTOBER

12

REGARDLESS OF YOUR circumstances you can choose joy and refuse misery!

GIVING IS A great antidote for greed. "Sometimes you can become rich by being generous or poor by being greedy. Generosity will be rewarded: give a cup of water, and you will receive a cup of water in return." Proverbs 11:24–25

"I PRAY TO YOU, Lord! Please listen. Don't hide from me in my time of trouble. Pay attention to my prayer and quickly give an answer." Psalm 102:1–2

"Money is something we choose to trade our life energy for. Our life energy is our allotment of time here on earth, the hours of precious life available to us…it is limited and irregular…our choices about how we use it express the meaning and purpose of our time here on earth."
— Joe Dominguez and Vicki Robin

IF YOUR EMPLOYER offers a 401(k) plan, participate at
the maximum level allowed. It's not often Uncle Sam offers
you such a wonderful gift, so take full advantage of it.

"I'VE GOT ALL the money I'll ever need—if I die by 4 o'clock." — Henny Youngman

WHEN PAINTING A home for resale, paint it yellow. Statistics say this will give you a decided advantage over similar homes in the same neighborhood.

IF YOU HAVE the opportunity to join a federally insured credit union, you absolutely should.

OCTOBER

DIRECT DEPOSIT OF your paycheck into your bank account is a safe, quick, convenient and smart way to manage your cash.

THERE IS SOMETHING about the act of giving that cannot be explained in purely rational terms. I believe with all my heart that the act of giving invites God's supernatural intervention into our lives and our finances. I don't know about you but the idea of opening my life to that kind of power is too awesome to miss.

THE GOAL OF an automatic investment plan is to make it very difficult to avoid saving. Just like diets, budgets don't work. The successful alternative to a budget is a plan, a blueprint for your financial future. I love the concept of a plan. With plans cities are built, battles are won and chaos is turned to order.

PART OF ALL the money that flows into my life is mine
to keep; I pay God first, myself second, and others third.

Living on credit can be hazardous to your future.

NOT ALL BANKS are created equal. Comparison shop to find the one with low or free checking accounts, minimal fees and most generous fringe benefits.

OCTOBER

5

During the spring, summer and fall whenever you pick wildflowers or buy a bouquet of flowers or are given roses, think ahead to Christmas. Dried flowers make beautiful additions to packages, wreaths, garlands and topiary.

MARCH 29

No MATTER WHAT, don't give up!

4

IT DOESN'T MATTER how much money you make. Millionaires go bankrupt every day. The problem isn't what they earn, it's what they do with what they've got.

MARCH

MOST OF OUR problems in handling money stem
from unexamined patterns rather than from uncontrollable
urges.

"THERE WAS A time when a fool and his money were soon parted, but now it happens to everybody."
— Adlai Stevenson

MARCH

31

"Money is like an arm or a leg—use it or lose it!"
— Henry Ford

OCTOBER

2

THERE IS NOTHING like the feeling of not owing anybody anything. Having a car that's paid off, no balances on your credit cards and no personal loans–now that's financial freedom!

APRIL

1

"FINANCIAL SECURITY IS that point in time when you can live the lifestyle you have chosen, financed from the assets you have accumulated, without the need for any additional income." — Alvin Danenberg, CFP, DDS

WOMEN LIVE AN average of seven years longer than men. — U.S. National Center for Health Statistics

2

FINANCIALLY CONFIDENT WOMEN think first and spend later.

SEPTEMBER

WHINING DOESN'T SOLVE problems.

INVESTING MEANS TO put money to use by purchase or expenditure in something offering profitable returns. Investing is an active and dynamic process. A wise investor always holds the safety of her investment dollars to be of the utmost importance.

SEPTEMBER

FINANCIALLY CONFIDENT WOMEN refuse to live under the fantasy of entitlement.

THERE MUST BE more to life than having everything. "Don't store up treasures on earth! Moths and rust can destroy them and thieves can break in and steal them. Instead, store up your treasure in heaven where moths and rust cannot destroy them and thieves cannot break in and steal them. Your heart will always be where your treasure is." Matthew 6:19–21.

IT IS VERY easy to confuse having with being.
Contrary to popular belief, you are *not what you drive.*

THE PHENOMENON OF credit cards has all but destroyed the importance of delayed gratification. There's something nice about the longing and yearning that accompanies having to wait. "A longing fulfilled is sweet to the soul." Proverbs 13:19, NIV

SOMETIMES IT SEEMS like mail order catalogs have nearly taken over the country. My mailbox is gone and a mini-mall has sprung up in its place!

YOU CANNOT PAY off your credit-card bill by putting it on your credit card!

"Don't FALL IN love with money. Be satisfied with what you have. The Lord has promised that he will not leave us or desert us." Hebrews 13:5

"NEITHER A BORROWER nor a lender be; For loan oft loses both itself and friend." –*Hamlet*, Act I, scene 3.

SEPTEMBER

IN A NATIONWIDE survey of 1,018 women 50 percent said they were solely responsible for balancing the checkbook, 56 percent said they had sole responsibility for paying bills and 38 percent said they were responsible for developing and maintaining the family budget.
— Oppenheimer Management Corporation

APRIL

A NICKEL GOES A long way now. You can carry it around for days without finding a thing it will buy.

24

"IT'S BETTER TO obey the Lord and have only a little, than to be very rich and terribly confused." Proverbs 15:16

No ANTIDOTE FOR overspending is more effective and immediate than saving money.

SEPTEMBER

23

"NEVER ASK OF money spent where the spender thinks it went." — Robert Frost.

CREDIT CARD DEBT getting you down? Maybe it's time for a little plastic surgery.

LIVING ON CREDIT keeps one locked in the past.

APRIL

11

THE IDEAL STRATEGY is to get out of debt faster than
the speed of worry.

Raw egg whites will remove chewing gum from anything, including hair, without leaving a trace.

IF YOU WOULD know the value of money, try to borrow some. — Benjamin Franklin

SEPTEMBER

VIEW CHANGE AS one of life's constants. Welcome it. Expect it. Anticipate it. "Christ gives me the strength to face anything!" Philippians 4:13

APRIL   13

CLEARING AWAY THE dark clouds of financial
oppression will release joy, passion and excitement in your
life.

YOU HAVE TWO choices: Accept conditions as they exist or accept the responsibility for changing them.

Store opened containers of sour cream and cottage cheese upside down in the refrigerator. This will double their useful life.

LET FAILURE BE your teacher not your undertaker.

APRIL

15

"WHO YOU ARE speaks so loudly I can't hear what you're saying." — Ralph Waldo Emerson

WHEN YOU ARE in the valley keep the goal firmly in view and you will get the renewed energy to continue to climb.

THE REASON MANY people don't live within their means is because they don't consider that living.

SEPTEMBER

16

D ON'T BE A compulsive hoarder or a compulsive spender. Give, save, plan, anticipate and then live life to its fullest! "You cannot serve God and money." Luke 16:13

NEVER BEFORE IN the history of this country has credit been so available and debt so attractive.

IT'S ALL TOO easy to neglect the important and give in to the urgent.

A STACK OF 1,000 dollars bills is about 3 3/4-inches high; $4.77 trillion (roughly the national debt) would make a stack of one dollar bills 282,000 miles high. The moon is 239,000 miles away so our national debt in dollar bills is about 43,000 miles beyond the moon!

SEPTEMBER

Seventy-two percent of adult women were employed in 1995 versus 29 percent in 1955. — U.S. Department of Commerce. U.S. Bureau of Labor Statistics

YOU'D BE SURPRISED how much it costs to look this cheap. — Dolly Parton

STOP RATIONALIZING, stop stewing. Get up out of your chair and start doing!

APRIL

MAKE SURE YOUR one all-purpose credit card is one with no annual feel and a twenty-five day grace period. The interest rate should be of little consequence since you will never pay interest, ideally.

SEPTEMBER

12

IT'S NOT TOO LATE to start listening to the quietest whisperings of your heart. It's not too late to start fulfilling your dreams!

SHARE A MAGAZINE with a friend or neighbor and save 50 percent every time!

SEPTEMBER

11

COURAGE MEANS TO stay focused during stressful periods.

To ERR IS human
But this you should learn
Don't be human on your tax return.

"The Lord hates anyone who cheats, but he likes everyone who is honest." Proverbs 11:1

SEPTEMBER

"GOD CARES FOR you so turn all you worries over to him." I Peter 5:7

"YOU CAN LIVE well if you're rich and you can live
well if you're poor, but if you're poor, it's much cheaper."
— Andrew Tobias, Author

PERMA-DEBT: Rolling debt over from month to month, making only the minimum payments and keeping balances close to, or at the maximum.

THE LOVE OF MONEY causes all kinds of trouble. Some people want money so much that they have given up their faith and caused themselves a lot of pain. I Timothy 6:10

WITH DETERMINATION AND commitment the majority of financial situations can be turned around quickly.

APRIL

25

WHOEVER LOVES MONEY never has enough money; whoever loves wealth is never satisfied with his income.
Ecclesiastes 5:10, NIV

THE BIGGEST REASON women find themselves in financial difficulty is not because they don't have enough money; it's because they don't know how to control their spending.

APRIL 26

Money can't buy friends but it can get you a better class of enemy.

SEPTEMBER

D ON'T LOOK AT the 60 cents you spend each day at the soft drink machine as just 60 cents. Buy your favorite soft drink in bulk at 25 cents a can and bring your own. Look at it as not spending 35 cents a day times 5 days a week, which equals $1.75 a week or $87 a year or $2,610 over one's career.

"In God we trust—all others pay cash."
— Sign in an Arkansas diner

A HOME MORTGAGE SHOULD be paid off during one's working years and prior to retirement. The security of knowing you have a place to live free from rent or monthly payment is a retirement gift you need to give yourself.

ANY FOOL can spend but it takes someone with real character to save.

SEPTEMBER

4

THE WINTER SEASON of my life will arrive on time whether I'm prepared or not. Clearly, being prepared beats the alternative.

APRIL

29

CHECK THE LABEL before making a clothing purchase. "Dry clean only" is going to double or triple the effective cost of the garment.

"GROW OLD ALONG with me!
The best is yet to be,
The last of life, for which the first was made:
Our times are in His hand
Who saith, "A whole I planned,
Youth shows but half; trust God; see all nor be afraid!"

— Robert Browning

Experience teaches you to recognize a mistake when you've made it again.

2

AN EMERGENCY FUND is mandatory to keep me financially viable during those seasons when my cash flow is cut off.

"WITH ALL YOUR heart you must trust the Lord and not your own judgment. Always let him lead you and he will clear the road for you to follow." Proverbs 3: 5–6

SEPTEMBER

1

THE BEST WAY out is always through.
— Robert Frost

MAY

2

KNOWING MY EXACT financial condition lifts the fog and allows me to focus on my financial goals.

KEEP A SPENDING record. Seeing where your money goes will keep you from lapsing into a spending coma.

MAY

3

Don't carry much cash. If you leave your credit card, debit card, ATM card, checkbook and most of your cash at home it will be very difficult to make unplanned purchases.

AUGUST

30

"I'm living so far beyond my income that we may almost be said to be living apart." e.e. cummings

MAY

4

COMMON SENSE IN an uncommon degree is what the world calls wisdom. "Wisdom is more powerful than weapons." Ecclesiastes 9:18

No MATTER WHAT your particular calling in life as a mother, career woman, wife or grandmother–you're a woman both wonderful and unique.

By AND LARGE, mothers and housewives are the only workers who do not have regular time off. They are the great vacationless class. — Ann Morrow Lindbergh

AUGUST

28

"WORK BRINGS PROFIT; talk brings poverty."
— Proverbs 14:23

THERE'S ONLY ONE way to accumulate money. You must have more money coming in than going out.

"LITTLE DROPS OF water wear down big stones."
— Russian Proverb

JUST BECAUSE YOU'RE going shopping doesn't mean you have to come home with something.

CALL THE SOCIAL Security Administration at 1–800–772–1213 and ask for a request form. Send it in and within three weeks you'll have a printout that shows your earnings for every year you've ever worked plus an estimate of your benefits at various retirement ages.

MAY 8

Wᴀɪᴛ ᴀ ʟɪᴛᴛʟᴇ longer and perhaps you'll see you don't need it.

FRUGALITY SIMPLY MEANS striving to get the very best
value you can for each dollar you spend and fully enjoying
the things you have or make use of.

Well, you just listen to me, Buster, I can't be overdrawn because I still have checks!

Don't kid yourself, buying on sale isn't saving. It's spending.

KEEP A SET of jumper cables in your car. In the case of a dead battery your cables might surely save you the cost of an expensive service call.

THOSE THINGS THAT hurt, instruct.
— Benjamin Franklin

THE FIRST LAW of economics: You can't have a filet mignon life on a bologna income.

"LIVING BENEATH YOUR means is the only route to take to enjoy a secure and comfortable standard of living throughout your working and retirement years. Living beneath your means isn't a suggestion. It's an imperative. Spend less than you earn!" — Jonathan Pond, author

SOME WOMAN ARE compelled to make financial changes not because they finally see the light but because they feel the heat.

FINANCIALLY CONFIDENT WOMEN know precisely their financial condition.

WHY IS THERE always so much month left at the end of the money?

IT IS BETTER to be prepared for an opportunity and not have one than to have an opportunity and not be prepared.

USE BAKING SODA. It's cheap and as a non-abrasive scouring powder it cleans and shines chrome, keeps drains from clogging, removes hard-water marks, cleans plastic, removes odors, degreases, cleans fiberglass, removes crayon stains from washable walls, and when added (1/2 cup per load) to laundry with liquid detergent, greatly improves effectiveness.

IT'S EASY TO meet expenses. Everywhere we go, there they are.

WANT TO ESTIMATE the cost of living? Take your present income and add twenty percent.

AUGUST

18

OBSTACLES ARE THOSE frightful things you see when you take your eyes off your goal. — Henry Ford

BUDGET: A family's attempt to live below its yearnings.

THE UNITED STATES has an estimated 17 square feet of shopping center space per person. From 1960 to 1980 the number of shopping centers grew from 3,000 to 20,000.

FACE it: Your yearning power will always exceed your earning power.

INVESTMENT SEMINARS CAN be very beneficial. Consider attending a seminar sponsored by a major financial institution. They are less likely to be disguised sales pitches than ones from little-known groups.

MAY

18

SECURITY IS NOT measured by the things you have but rather by the things you can do without.

SUCCESSFUL LIVING IS like a violin. It must be practiced every day.

MAY

19

TODAY IS THE tomorrow you worried about yesterday–and all is well. — Corrie Ten Boom

AUGUST

14

$\mathbb{S}$ING *Amazing Grace* today, all five verses if you know them. It will lift your spirits!

20

COFFEE BEANS AND ground coffee retain their strong flavor and freshness longer if stored in the freezer.

IT'S FAR EASIER to stay out of debt than to get out of debt.

Eighty percent of Americans have never had a savings account.

AUGUST

12

You SHOULDN'T GO through life with a catcher's mitt on both hands. You need to be able to throw something back!

There is no better way to demonstrate to the world that you are not a person of integrity than to bounce a check.

Beyond a certain comfortable style of living, the more material things you have the less freedom you have.

THE TIME IT takes to repay a debt is inversely proportional to the time it took to do the damage.

I HAVE LEARNED THAT when your husband cooks you should compliment everything he fixes.

MAY

24

FINANCIALLY CONFIDENT WOMEN save money consistently.

IF YOU LOSE the back piece of a pierced earring, break or cut the eraser from a pencil and insert it on the post for a temporary fix-it.

IT'S EASIER to act your way into a feeling than to feel your way into an action.

THE BEST WAY to lose a friend is to lend her money.

SIMPLIFYING, even when done in a tiny way, has the ability to refresh the soul. You won't believe all the extra time and freedom you'll enjoy, to say nothing of the positive effect on your bank account.

MAY

27

Do your best with what you have.

THE DEGREE OF a woman's financial confidence greatly determines her success.

WHEN IT COMES to food, buy what's in season. It takes a little research to know what's coming into season and what's not. Out-of-season produce is the most expensive. Stick to what's plentiful and therefore cheaper.

NEVER GO GROCERY shopping when you're hungry,
when you're exhausted or without a written list.

COSTROPHOBIA: Having to buy something simply because it's on sale.

IT'S NOT WHAT happens to you that is important. It's what you do about it.

MAY   30

How few our real needs, how vast our imaginary ones.

AUGUST

3

At LEAST ONCE a year you should order your personal credit reports. The big three bureaus are: TRW 800–392–1122; Equifax 800–685–1111; TransUnion 800–916–8800. Call for specific information.

"IT IS POOR judgment to countersign another's note, to become responsible for his debts." Proverbs 17:18

NOTHING OF VALUE comes without effort.

JUNE

1

Work on your marriage. Divorce is very expensive.

1

No MATTER HOW much you hear and read, no one has a clue about what the stock market is going to do.

JUNE

2

EMBRACE LIFE'S CHALLENGES. Kites rise against the wind, not with it.

JULY

31

Most of the things we worry about never happen!

UNLESS THE DEBT spiral is halted, a woman's chance of every getting out of financial bondage are slim to none.

IF YOU PLAN to remodel, remember this unbending rule: It will cost twice as much and take twice as long as you thought it would.

SHE WHO HESITATES, saves money!

LIFE IS LIKE a bicycle; not much happens unless you do some pedaling.

MOST OF US would be willing to pay as we go, if we could just finish paying for where we've been.

No MATTER YOUR age, start a retirement plan.

IN BIBLICAL TIMES, a man could have as many wives
as he could afford. Just like today.

Consignment shopping has become a very respectable way to purchase fine clothing at a fraction of the price. Look in your Yellow Pages under Clothing, consignment.

JUNE 7

A WOMAN IS LIKE a tea bag; you don't know her strength until she's in hot water. — Nancy Reagan

26

FIND A WAY to serve others and your life will have meaning.

LET GO OF things you can't have anyway.

ASK YOURSELF WHAT you would do with your life if money were not a consideration. Perhaps you can find a way to do that now.

HOPE IS the feeling you have that the feeling you have isn't permanent. — Jean Kerr "I will bless you with a future filled with hope—a future of success, not of suffering." Jeremiah 29:11

JULY

24

KEEP TRACK OF where your money is going.

JUNE

10

IN SPITE of the cost of living, it's still popular.
— Kathleen Norris, Nineteenth-Century Novelist

Make people more important than possessions.

There is nothing so habit-forming as money.

"WHETHER YOU THINK you can or think you can't, you're right." — Henry Ford

JUNE

12

THE SECRET OF staying young is to live honestly, eat slowly, sleep sufficiently, work industriously, worship faithfully—and then lie about your age. — Lucille Ball

FIND SOMETHING YOU can do better than anyone you know. Take things step-by-step. It's easier to get to the fifth rung of a ladder after you've climbed the first four.

NEXT TO SOUND judgment, diamonds and pearls are the rarest things in the world.
— Jean de La Bruyère, 1645

JULY

DON'T WASTE TIME regretting the past.

14

TIME IS GOD'S way of keeping everything from happening at once.

If you can't change the situation, change your attitude toward it.

JUNE

15

IT HELPS TO think sacrifice, not deprivation. Sacrifice means to give up something of value for the sake of something else that is more important or more worthy. Deprivation means to have a freedom or enjoyment taken away. Sacrifice focuses on a goal. Deprivation focuses on poor me.

18

NEVER INVEST IN coins, precious metals or the futures markets even if you think you understand them.

JUNE

16

BETTER A LITTLE caution than a great regret.

Do you realize we are paying for things we no longer have with money we don't have yet?

JUNE

17

BEFORE MARRIAGE THE three little words are "I love you;" after marriage they are "Let's eat out."

GIVE MORE THAN you take.

How much difference can $5 make, anyway? A $1,000 credit card balance at 17 percent interest with fixed monthly payments of $15 takes more than 205 months (17 years) to be repaid (total payback $3,082). Increasing that monthly payment to $20 pays the balance in 87 months (7 years) with a total payback of $1,750.

JULY

15

START a "victory" journal and write down every success you have.

JUNE

19

A HOME-BASED ENTREPRENEUR IS a self-employed person working 18 hours a day to avoid working 8 hours for someone else.

"TOUGH TIMES DON'T last but tough people do."
— Old Texas Proverb

Break down big challenges into little pieces. Then do them one by one.

13

WHEN YOU CHANGE the batteries in your smoke
detectors every six months, don't throw them away. They still
have lots of life remaining and can be used in radios,
beepers and toys.

PEOPLE WHO SAY it cannot be done should not interrupt those who are doing it.

DON'T CHARGE ANYTHING that is down the drain before you get the bill.

JUNE

22

DEAR FATHER, Hardly a day goes by that I'm not bombarded with tempting offers to conform to society's ideas of what I need to be happy. Renew my mind so that I always find my contentment and security in You, not in the false security the world offers. Amen.

JULY

11

In my home, she who does the laundry keeps the cash.
Keep a bank with your laundry supplies and as the coins
and bills make it through the cycle, stash 'em!

BUYING IN BULK is a great way to stretch the dollars…provided you can consume all of it before it goes bad!

Ashes from a wood-burning stove or fireplace make wonderful fertilizer for rose bushes.

"ONLY THE MEDIOCRE are always at their best."
— Jean Giraudoux, 1882

ACCORDING TO THE National Center for Women and Retirement Research, the average age of widowhood is 56 and 75 percent of the elderly poor are women.

"VENI, VIDI, VISA. Interpretation: We came, we saw, we went shopping." — Jan Barrett

JULY

GENEROUS PEOPLE SELDOM have emotional and mental problems.

JUNE

26

Money is better than poverty, if only for financial reasons. — Woody Allen

"To EVERYTHING THERE is a season and a time to every purpose under the heaven….A time to get and a time to lose; a time to keep and a time to cast away….Ecclesiastes 3:1,6

27

I<small>F THE GRASS</small> always looks greener on the other side of the fence, learn to enjoy yellow grass. "I have learned in whatsoever state I am, therewith to be content." Philippians 4:11, KJV

Is YOUR HOME a place of calm and peace or a burial ground for junk and clutter? "De-junking is the cheapest, fastest and most effective way to become physically and financially sound, emotionally and intellectually happy.... Remember, everything has a cost to acquire and to maintain and most of that cost is your time and energy."

— Don Aslett, author.

JUNE

28

ALMOST HALF OF the twelve million Americans who
run full-time businesses from their homes are women.

MAKE THE DIRTIEST windows sparkle by washing them with a wet sponge sprinkled with a bit of baking soda. Rinse the window with a clean sponge and dry with towels or squeegee.

NEED MEDICAL INFORMATION? Call Nurse-On-Call, 800–801–2273, 7am - 11pm EST, 7 days a week to ask an RN your questions. This service is free of charge.

NEVER USE YOUR credit card for a cash advance. On the typical cash advance you end up paying an effective rate of 33 percent interest.

According to Consumer Reports the lowly cheap brands of shampoo found in the drug or grocery store rated just as high as the pricey salon brands.

JULY

3

Set aside money to use only for having fun.

NEED A FREE knee patch for a pair of pants? Steal the back pocket. It matches every time.

FINANCIALLY CONFIDENT WOMEN don't see the monthly payment but focus instead on the total price tag.